Rosary Meditations
and
Care for Creation

Petitions and Supplications
for Mother Earth

Mary Jane Miller

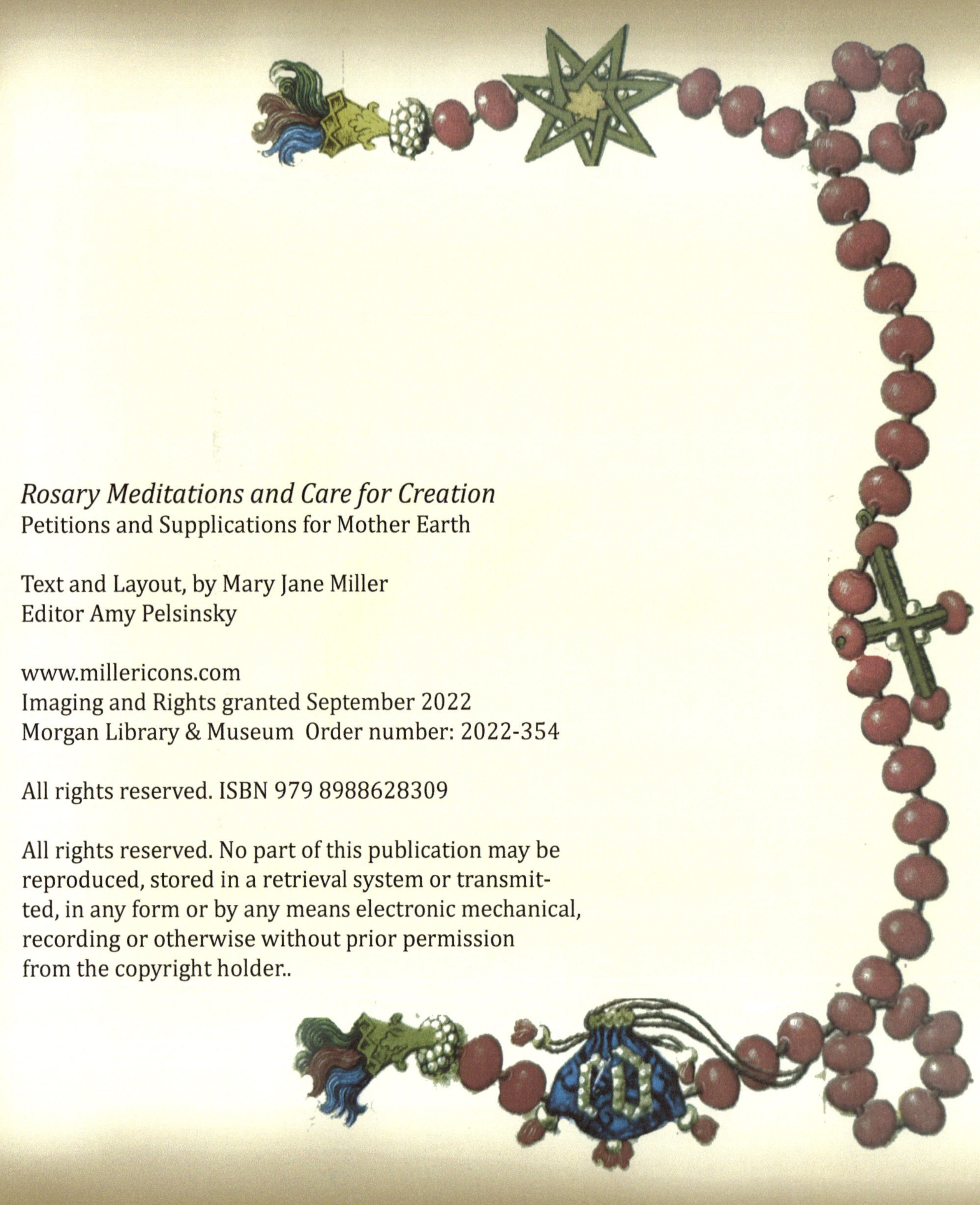

Rosary Meditations and Care for Creation
Petitions and Supplications for Mother Earth

Text and Layout, by Mary Jane Miller
Editor Amy Pelsinsky

www.millericons.com
Imaging and Rights granted September 2022
Morgan Library & Museum Order number: 2022-354

Introduction

Praying the Rosary is familiar to most Christians. If you are Catholic, no doubt you have arrived at Mass on a weekday at early dawn and heard the rhythmic recitation of this sacred prayer. Maybe at some point you have been quietly praying alone, and a small group of two or three come into the sanctuary and begin cantillating without pause. The sound drifts unconstrained from one corner of the sanctuary to another. You may have traveled to a foreign country, stopped in at a church, and seen a woman murmuring
with a string of beads and wondered, to whom does she speak?

On my street here in San Miguel de Allende, Mexico, a woman we call
'the taquera' gathers 10 to 15 people every Wednesday night in her garage. They sit casually and recite the entire Rosary so fast it is over in 20 minutes.
They produce a blur of intercession for humanity as they recite.

The Rosary has been a principle prayer form used for the sick, those in need, and those in peril. Today, our Earth is sick, and she is in peril and needs our prayers. Christianity has tried to teach humanity how to be human for 2,000 years. The clergy have left little deference to the created order.
We have left that in God's hands.

On May 13, 2021, Pope Francis encouraged Christians around the world to pray the Rosary. He instructed believers to use the practice as an aid to better understand humanity's place on the planet and in the world. He said, "The Blessed Mother's intercession on behalf of Mother Earth can bring humanity to realize more deeply
the love God bestowed on Earth for our benefit".

Pope John Paul II compelled Catholics throughout his 27-year papacy to care for creation and to undergo an "ecological conversion". He often made time for outdoor recreation like hiking and skiing in his native Poland and elsewhere. In 2001, he said: "If we scan the regions of our planet, we immediately see that humanity has disappointed God's expectations. Man, especially in our time, has without hesitation devastated wooded plains and valleys, polluted waters, disfigured the earth's habitat, and made the air unbreathable. We must therefore encourage and support the 'ecological conversion,' for humanity to become more sensitive to the catastrophe to which we are heading."

I used to walk in the Mexican desert with a nun reciting the Rosary on Wednesdays. As the beads swung rhythmically with each step, I was at peace. Part of me wanted to stop the recitation and walk in silent reverence.

I have written new Rosary Meditations and Care for Creation, to highlight and focus on making us better servants of the environment. Mother Mary is still our intercessor and guide. Through her and these prayers, we ask for God's continued intercession on Earth for our benefit.

Mary is a creator with God, and she knows the magnificent, mysterious love that God created in her being. Let us learn from her and continue to celebrate and enjoy what God handed into our possession. The wisdom traditions throughout world religions have used the divine mother and the mystery of motherhood to unify their communities. Humanity's capacity to nurture is unsurpassed. We love with no limit and believe God has given us sovereign rule over all of creation. We have the responsibility to love and protect what has been given but did not create.

Meditations on Mystery

The word Rosary comes from the Latin rosarius, which means garland, bouquet, or "crown of roses". When spoken softly, the rosary is a spiritual bouquet of prayer, petals offered to Mother Mary. They are personal petitions on behalf of the wrong done during people's lives on Earth.

We call the prayer a 'Rosa' ary for its significant symbolism. Spiritually, the elegant rose offers a glimpse of a masterful Creator's presence in motion. They unfold from a small bud and open themselves in an array of many petals, like a lotus. It happens gradually, the way spiritual wisdom unfolds in people's lives. They bloom with dignity on a stem of thorns with a three-petal leaf that reminds us of the Holy Trinity

Roses emit a sweet fragrance, commonly used in perfumes. It is no wonder the delicate fragrance provokes thoughts of miracles and encounters with angels. In the Middle Ages, roses were hung from the ceilings of meeting rooms during special events. It was understood that everyone under the roses was sworn to confidentiality. Rosewater has anti-inflammatory and antioxidant properties and can hydrate our skin.

Rose hips, the fruit of roses, are beneficial when eaten for their high content of vitamin C.

Roses have a powerful energy field that vibrates
at a high electrical frequency—the highest of any flower on Earth.

The rose is a universal symbol of love that crosses many cultures. Pagans use roses as decorations to represent their hearts. Muslims view roses as symbols of the human soul, and smelling the scent of a rose reminds them of their spirituality. Hindus and Buddhists see roses and other flowers as expressions of spiritual joy. Egyptians used wreaths of roses heaped upon the tombs in the pyramids. In Greek mythology, roses are particularly associated with Aphrodite, the goddess of love. One legend tells that the first roses sprang from her tears, while another says the rose was a gift for gods to celebrate her rising from the sea.

Under Christianity, the foremost personification of the Divine Feminine was, of course, the Virgin Mary. The mysterious rose, sacred to Venus. Mary became associated with the original purity and uncorruptable beauty. She has been called the "mystic rose" or, the "rose without thorns '' because of her role as the tender mother of Jesus Christ.

Christians view roses as reminders of the Garden of Eden, a paradise in a world that reflected God's design before sin corrupted it. Tradition says that before the fall roses grew with no thorns. Thorns appeared after humanity was driven out.

At weddings, baptisms, marriages, and funerals, flower bouquets were given as visual prayers of devotion, contrition, and joy offered to God. Humanity plays a vital role in God's plan through sacramental acts and devotions. We particpate in redeeming a corrupted world and the unfolding of consciousness.

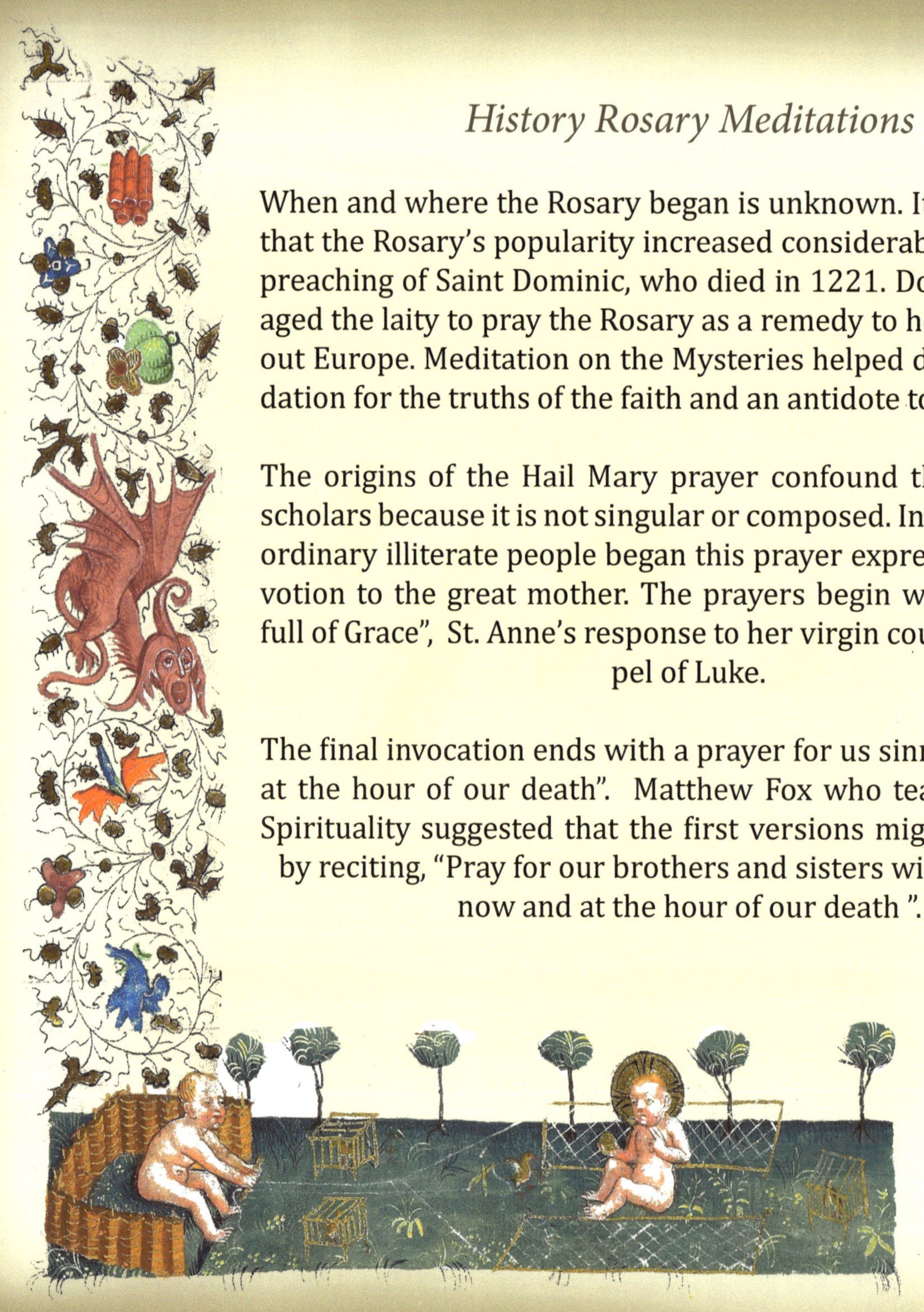

History Rosary Meditations

When and where the Rosary began is unknown. It is undeniable that the Rosary's popularity increased considerably through the preaching of Saint Dominic, who died in 1221. Dominic encouraged the laity to pray the Rosary as a remedy to heresy throughout Europe. Meditation on the Mysteries helped develop a foundation for the truths of the faith and an antidote to bad behavior.

The origins of the Hail Mary prayer confound the priests and scholars because it is not singular or composed. In the beginning, ordinary illiterate people began this prayer expressing their devotion to the great mother. The prayers begin with "Hail Mary full of Grace", St. Anne's response to her virgin cousin in the gospel of Luke.

The final invocation ends with a prayer for us sinners, "now and at the hour of our death". Matthew Fox who teaches Creation Spirituality suggested that the first versions might have ended by reciting, "Pray for our brothers and sisters with the angels, now and at the hour of our death ".

Rosary beads have a long history in the Catholic Church, and virtually every major religious tradition in the world uses some form of prayer beads. They come in every style of glass, wood, ceramic, or plastic and symbolize an ongoing commitment to prayer. For centuries, people around the world have used pebbles, a string of knots, or beads on a cord to keep track of prayer
mantras offered to God.

The chain of beads establishes a framework, a context, and an intention. The repetition serves as a foundation for uninterrupted meditation. These beads allow the one who prays to be still and quiet the mind. Using the rosary or prayer beads helps to bring us into contemplation—the presence of God—by engaging
our whole mind, body, and spirit.

Touching each successive bead aids us in keeping our emotions from wandering on two levels. One level is bringing our mind into stillness through the rhythm of vocal prayer. The second level engages our body through the continuity of touch with each bead. Regulating your breath during recitation
is a proven technique to stay in the moment.

The structure and flow of the prayer aids the individual through repetition and familiarity. As with the Lord's Prayer, we know it, and therefore, the mind can bloom in color with each phrase. The rhythm of the prayer quiets the spirit and helps a person be more receptive to hearing God and, thus, be transformed spiritually. The Rosary Meditations and Care for Creation, used as a sacrament, prayer, or devotion can be a tremendous aid in drawing us closer to God
and the Earth.

Pray for Our Planet Earth

In ancient scripture, the book of Genesis opens with humanity being given the whole Earth into our care. Early saints like St. Hildegard of Bingen, St.Thérèse of Lisieux, St. Benedict, St. Francis of Assisi, St. Kateri Tekakwitha, St. Aquinas, and Teilhard de Chardin all contemplated and exalted the wonder of Creation.

It is not redundant or inconsequential to pray for God's creation. Loving care for God's gift is not a monumental job, it only requires awareness. When we ask why we are here, and how we are shaping our terrestrial home, our honest conclusions might feel uncomfortable. It is prudent to ask,
"Have we been good stewards of this extraordinary planet?"

I hope the new text for this Rosary for our Planet Earth will help connect our hearts with the marvelous intelligence that has harmonized all of creation for our benefit. The new Rosary prayer stimulates the soul to become a receptive vessel, to make space to receive the in-pouring of Divine influence. Prayer and meditation are a time-tested method and tool for centering the mind.
Peace and compassion are essential for us,
more now than any other time in human history.

Through contemplating one mystery at a time, the depth of our adoration, contrition, thanksgiving, petition, and imagination is enriched.These five words have the power for healing our environmental crisis. Adoration, contrition, thanksgiving, petition, and imagination are urgent intentions
for our terrestrial home.

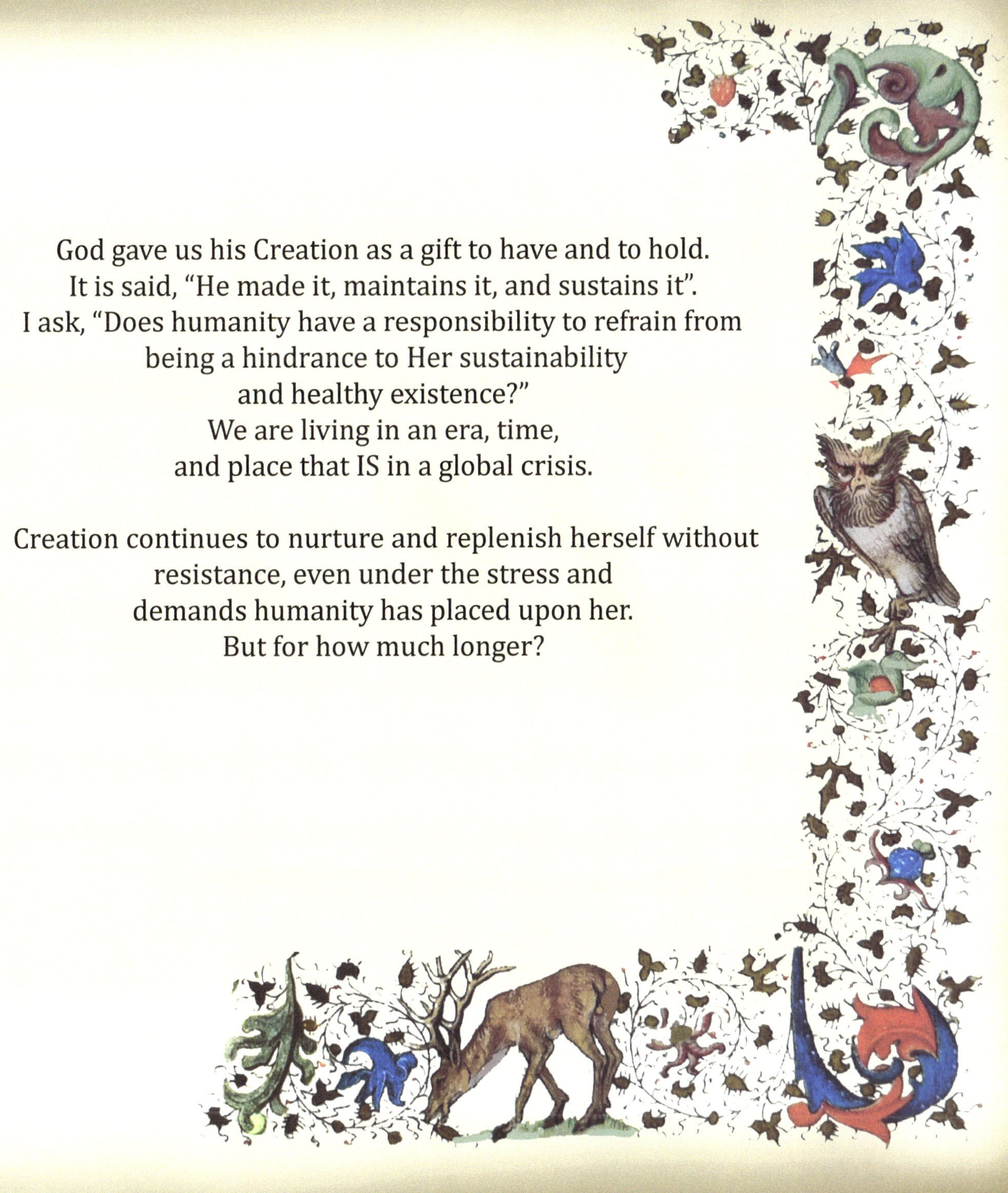

God gave us his Creation as a gift to have and to hold.
It is said, "He made it, maintains it, and sustains it".
I ask, "Does humanity have a responsibility to refrain from
being a hindrance to Her sustainability
and healthy existence?"
We are living in an era, time,
and place that IS in a global crisis.

Creation continues to nurture and replenish herself without
resistance, even under the stress and
demands humanity has placed upon her.
But for how much longer?

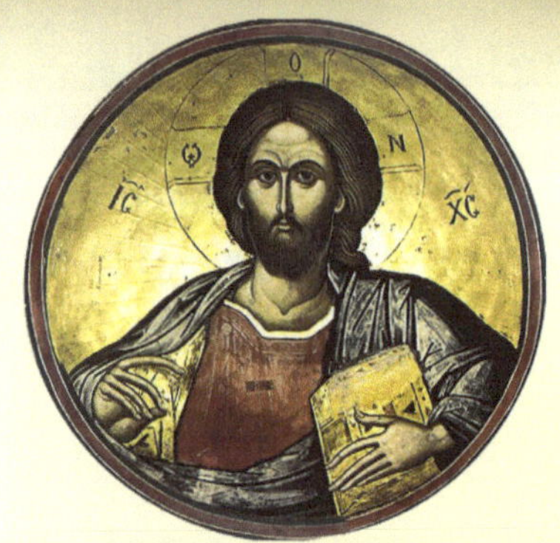

Rosary Meditations for each Mystery

Adoration - The Joyful Mysteries are the Annunciation, the Visitation, the Nativity, the Presentation of the Child Jesus, and the Finding of the Child Jesus in the Temple.

Contrition -The Sorrowful Mysteries comprise Christ's Agony in the Garden, the Scourging, the Crowning of Thorns, Carrying the Cross, and the Crucifixion.

Thanksgiving - The Luminous Mysteries comprise Christ's Baptism, the Wedding at Cana, the Proclamation of the Kingdom, the Transfiguration, and the Institution of the Eucharist.

Petition - The Glorious Mysteries include the Resurrection, the Ascension, the Descent of the Holy Spirit, the Assumption of Mary, and the Coronation of Mary.

Imagine - The Visual Mysteries complete the revelation and bring us back to dreaming about the perfection found in the Garden of Eden and hope for thy will be done on Earth as it is in Heaven.

Organize your Contemplative Prayer

Find a quiet place to rest and allow your body and mind to settle for a few minutes. After a short while, begin with the first prayer bead at an unhurried pace.
Allow the calm rhythm of your repetitions to deepen. You will hear the move-
ments of the Spirit. This book is formatted to use by the day,
by the week, all together, in a group, or alone.

Using a string of beads is a suggestion. You can buy a set in most catholic book
stores. Or collect a few special beads, deciding the number and size that suits
you. Catholic tradition uses ten repetitions; give yourself permission to format
the base prayer as you like.

Hail Mary, Full of Grace, The Lord is with thee. Blessed art thou among women,
and blessed is the fruit of thy womb, Jesus. Holy Mary, Mother of God, pray for
the Earth now, and at the hour of our death. Amen.

The large bead is called a cruciform bead. When you touch the large bead, read
the meditation in this book, giving yourself and others a chance to contem-
plate a phrase, word, or concept. Each of the five mysteries ends with the Lord's
Prayer. I have offered five versions from around the world. You can use any of
them or repeat the traditional version that has been
so beautifully recited for centuries.

Universal Wisdom used for a Paradigm Shift

Creation is not a one-time event, but a process of unfolding. Music communicates its beauty in many connected notes, a symphony of change and variation.The animals, insects, forests, fish in the sea, and beings that fly on wings are all living symphonies. Together we also create a harmonic resonance.

Humanity must work together in and with and under God in relationship and harmony with Nature. The time has come for us to stop what we're doing and face up to the consequenses we have ordained thinking we are separate from our maker. We, along with creation, shall all be gathered together and remain interconnected till the end.

We find ourselves caught in an illusion. We think riches and power can fulfill the longing we have to be part of and united to divine life. We are on the brink of a paradigm shift. We will join hands, breathe, and move together in a new way when we realize our connection to all of life. This era is redefining our place in relationship to everyone and every living creature. We cannot live outside the natural and spiritual laws that keep us alive. Let us pray for awareness.

These five meditations are based on the principal events in the Life of Jesus, using Mary as our intercessor. The mysteries knit together a short course in theology for their wealth of truth and inspiration contained within. The last and fifth meditation and mystery is for hope. Remarkably, the Holy Spirit does come through supplication, so believe our hearts and mind will receive unimaginable understanding and wisdom.

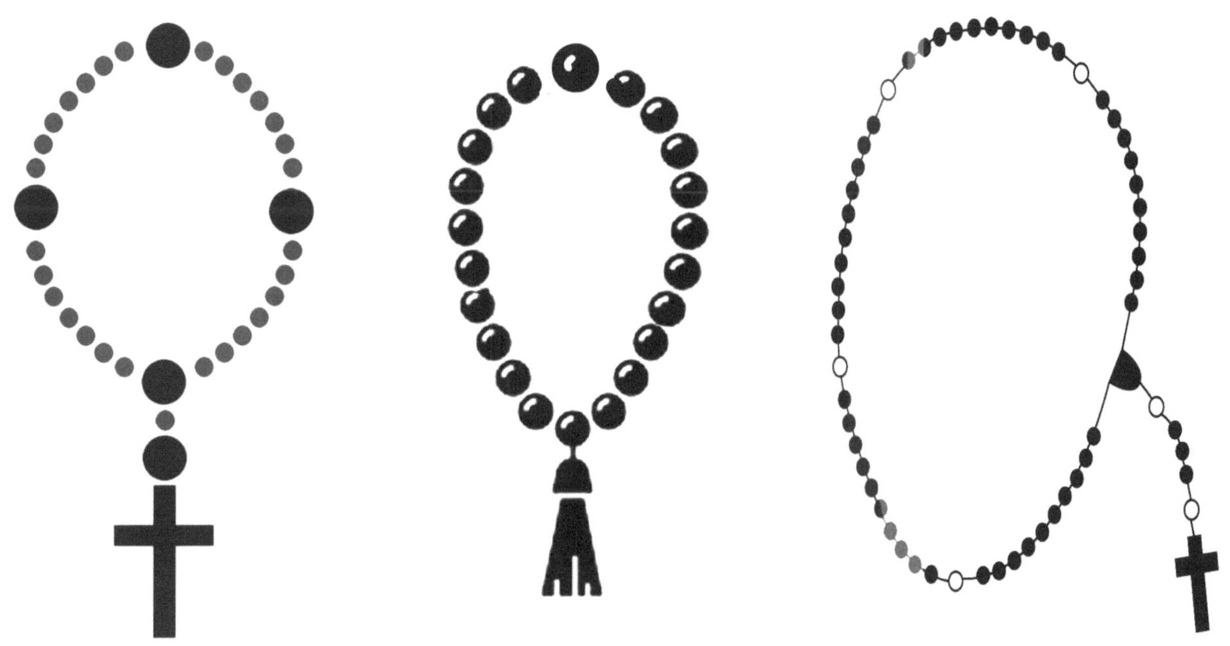

Let us Begin

Almighty Father, Creator of Heaven and Earth, in Christ,
our Lord, who was conceived by the Holy Spirit,
and born of the Virgin Mary,
grant us wisdom.

JOYFUL MYSTERIES

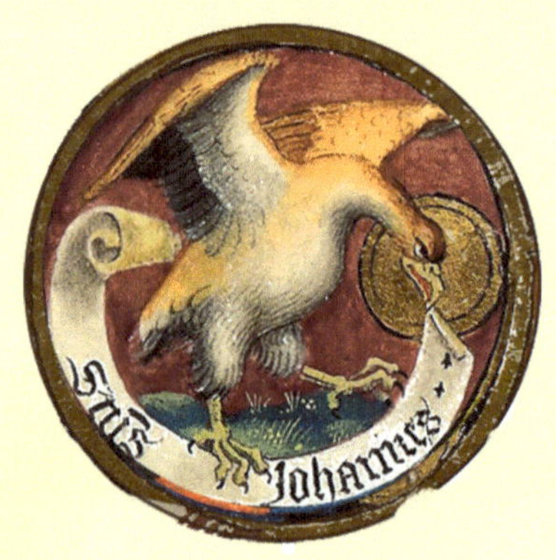

Rosary Meditations of Adoration

The Annunciation

Help us, to plumb the depths of stillness as witness to the quiet moment when Mary said Yes to God. Grant us the grace to listen and say Yes with Christ to love and respect God's glorious creation. May our Yes prompt us to follow God's laws that make all life possible.

Help us discern and understand His plan for life and revere thenatural order in all its abundance. Pray that we joyfully recognize with fresh eyes through inspired hearts all that has been given.

May our wombs will be filled with wisdom for the benefit of future generations. Mother Mary who, by your human act, gave birth to the most transcendent truth which is love.

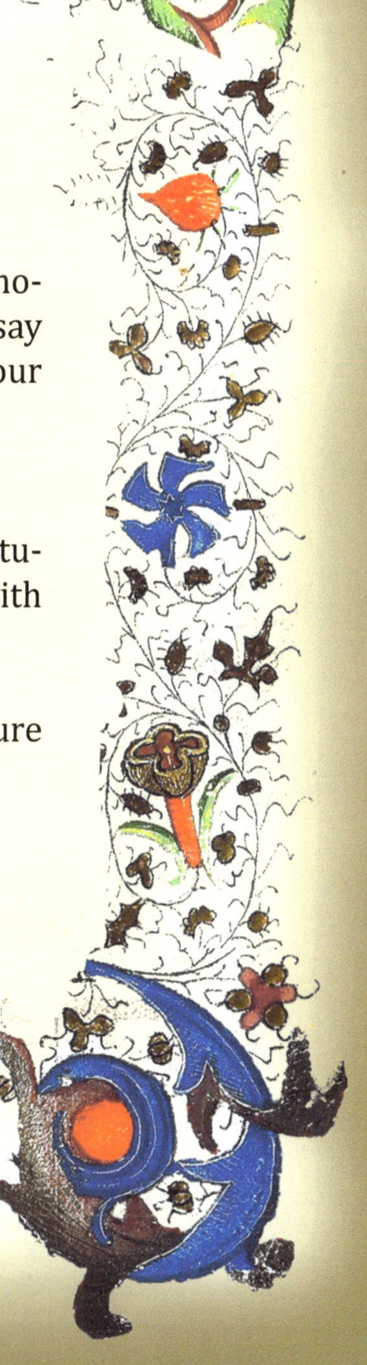

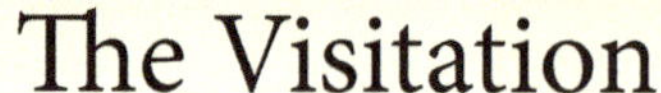

*Mary visits Elizabeth, who tells her
she will always be remembered.*

Help us, Mary. Grant us the grace to willingly share our time, resources and energy with all people. Help each of us to better know and live with Joy, knowing all of life is sacred.

We rejoice with Mary, and cherish every living creature on Earth down to the smallest microorganism. Guide us in being mindful of the potential for life around the globe. Let us not be a hindrance to others and allow all creatures to flourish.

We renew our desire to comfort the afflicted, strengthen what has become weak, and protect all that is born. Mother Mary who, by your human act, gave birth to the most transcendent truth which is love.

The Nativity

Jesus is born in a stable in Bethlehem.
Mary has birthed the light of God
and divine wisdom incarnate.

Mother Mary, Grant us the grace to birth Christ-likeness in the world. We have been born of One mind, regardless of circumstance. Let us rejoice in an authentic tenderness
for each breath of new life.

Mother, make us humble, with Jesus who shared his birthplace with that of the animals. Guide us to joyfully protect all life on every continent and realize our intimate kinship with all species.

Comfort and heal our illusion believing we are separate from the
natural biological process that is indivisible from the created
order. Mother Mary, who by your human act, gave birth
to the most transcendent truth which is love.

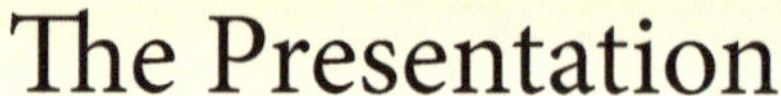

*Mary and Joseph take the infant Jesus
to the Temple to present him to God.*

Help us, Mary, that like you, we may make an offering of gratitude and service. May we hope that in doing so our souls in-
tuitively know how to protect all life and the world's abundant
resources. Pray for us to live our lives innocently before God.

Give us the strength and wisdom to teach our children the mag-
nificence of Creation. Our lives are vulnerable but
are made strong through the blessings of God, our Maker.

Grant us the grace to listen to and heed the words of those who
speak of faith in the future, who teach with scientific reason
and spiritual wisdom. Mother Mary, who by your human act,
gave birth to the most transcendent truth which is love.

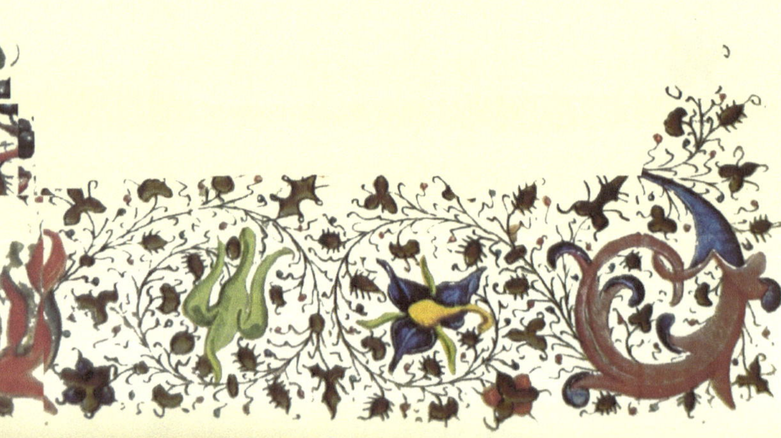

Finding Jesus
in the Temple

*Jesus is found in the Temple discussing his faith
with the teachers and elders.*

Grant us the grace to seek, to find, to listen, and to understand His truth.
Help us, Pray that the words of Jesus are on our lips
as we go about our day, opening discussions about
love for our planet.

The Lord teaches us to care for our sisters and brothers, encouraging
them to be stewards of the Earth's magnificent splendor. Help us discern
truth in all that Nature reveals. Let our leaders embrace a new-found joy
in preservation of resources and inter-related ecosystems
for our benefit and for the benefit of future generations.

Help us live as a united family with a common interest in global peace. In
doing so, we may live in harmony with Him, our neighbors, and all
Creation. Mother Mary, who by your human act, gave birth
to the most transcendent truth which is love.

OUR FATHER

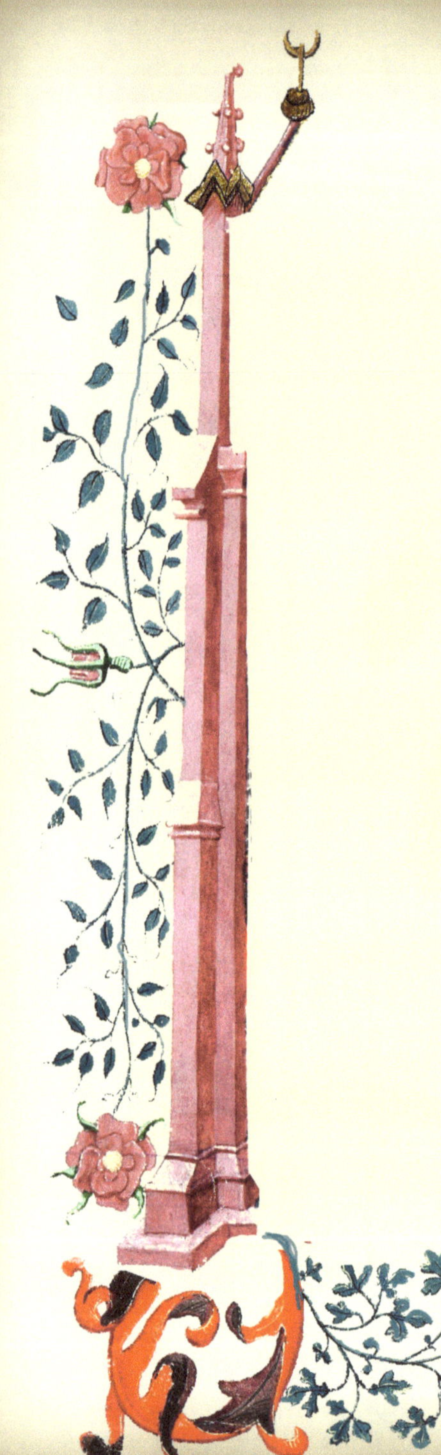

Our Father, who art in heaven,
hallowed be thy name;
thy kingdom come; thy will be done
on earth as it is in heaven.
Give us this day our daily bread;
and forgive us our trespasses
as we forgive those who trespass
against us;
lead us not into temptation,
but deliver us from evil.

Amen.

Sorrowful Mysteries

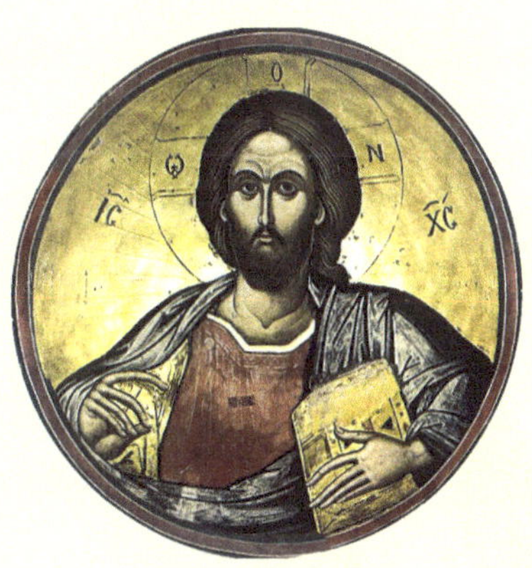

Meditations of Contrition

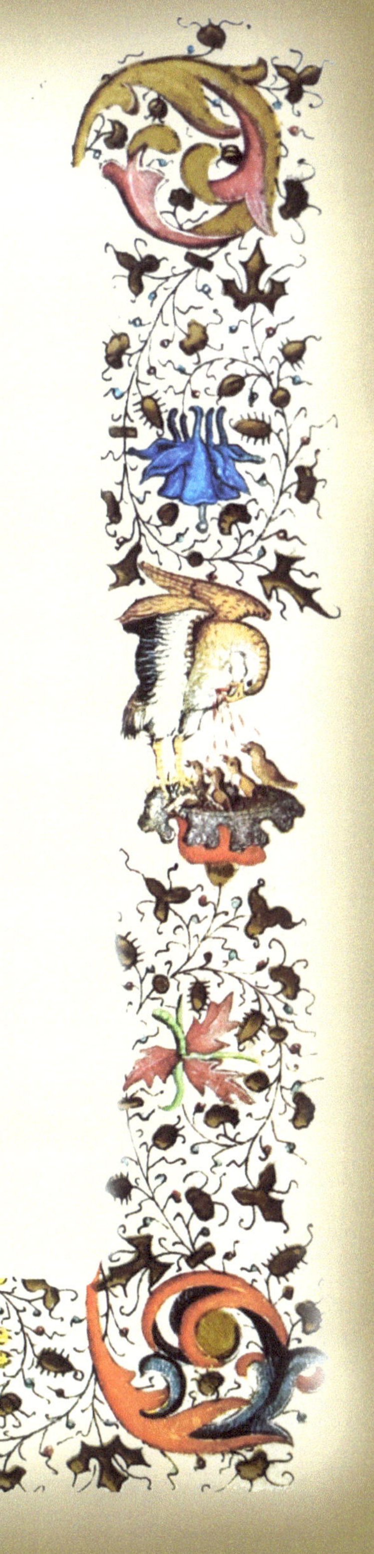

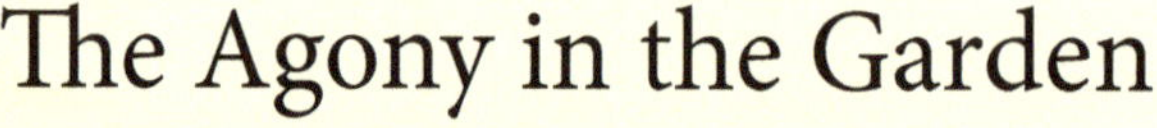

The Agony in the Garden

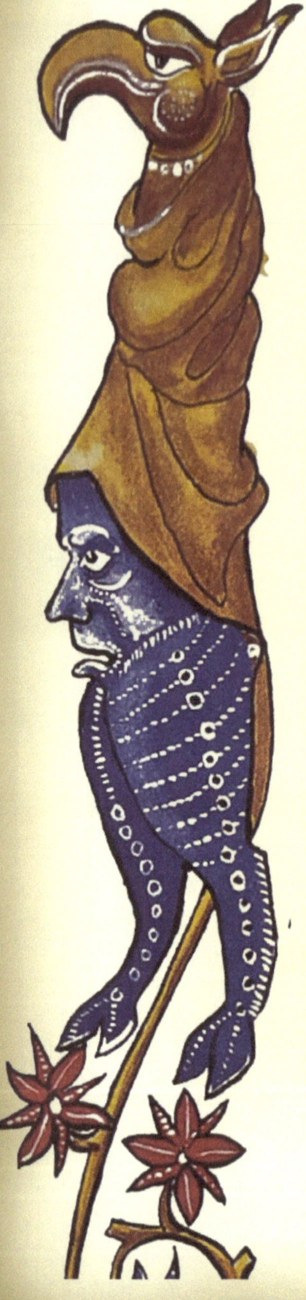

The disciples have fallen asleep, his teachings have exhausted them and they have lost consciousness in sleep. The Christ within each of us knows: "the hour is upon us." Jesus walked with us as a man and saw the face of humanity looking back at him.

Help us, Mother Mary, to admit with contrition that our choices and actions bring anguish to the world. Entering the garden with Peter, James, and John, Jesus prays, "My soul is sorrowful unto death."

As His hour approached, the many sins of the world weighed down your Son. We abandoned him in our sleep the night he prayed in the Garden of Gethsemane. He took on all of our ignorance—all the damages wrought by our vice, our indifference, and our refusal to follow God's laws.

Our worldly desires have corrupted cultures and the ecosystems that destroy life. We have brought to the world despair from our choices and unbridled desires. He has shown in Himself our guilt with contrition, "Father, if it be thy will, let the Earth be renewed."

The Scourging
at the Pillar

Jesus is lashed with whips.
The prophecy of Isaiah is fulfilled: "He was wouned
for our ungodliness, He was bruised for our sins."

Mother Mary, help the Church inspire every community to foster understanding without persecution or judgement. Pray that your Son grants us the grace to build political, social, corporate, and scientific systems to respect the dignity of life on Earth.

Help our leaders see beyond violence and aggression to rectify any injustice. Help us, Mother Mary, to show mercy for the indigenous, the immigrant, and the accused. Grant us courage to share the pain with Jesus in His scourging, the afflictions we have caused one another and on the whole world.

Comfort and heal the addictions and traumas that separate us from knowing we are loved and your love for us. He has shown in Himself our guilt with contrition. "Father, if it be thy will, let the Earth be renewed."

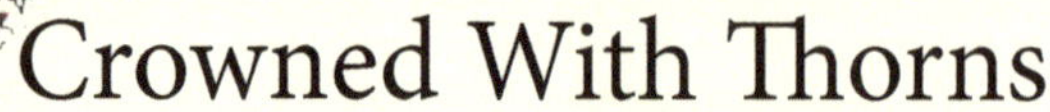

Jesus is mocked and crowned with thorns. "Behold what man has done to your creation!" Your Son and creation have been crucified at our own command, "Crucify Him! Crucify It!"

Help us, Mary, We have abandoned our Earth and have mocked its glory. Guide us in seeing clearly the damage being done to ourselves and future generations, as we watch with detachment the anguish of others. We are contrite for the sorrow we have caused that pierces your heart. Our humiliation is before us.

Help us to make choices that protect life and honor humanity and God's creation. Heal and comfort us—as individuals and as members of church, government, politics, and law enforcement— to respect the dignity of the human family. He has shown in Himself our guilt with contrition, "Father, if it be thy will, let the Earth be renewed."

Carrying the Cross

Jesus carries the cross that will be used to crucify him.
Have mercy on us and on the whole world.

Help us, Mary, to carry the cross for our behavior, having bruised and wounded our planet. Jesus speaks to the women: "Weep not for Me, but for yourselves and your children." Grant us the grace to see what we have done and rectify our ignorance by restoring the Earth's injured terrestrial body.

Mother Earth holds the untold anguish a Mother's Heart holds for her child. The women despaired as they watched His suffering. "If anyone is to be My disciple, let him take up his cross and follow Me." Mary, we are remorseful for our contribution to the swords of sorrow that pierced your heart and the Divine Earth.

He has shown in Himself our guilt with contrition,
"Father, if it be thy will, let the Earth be renewed."

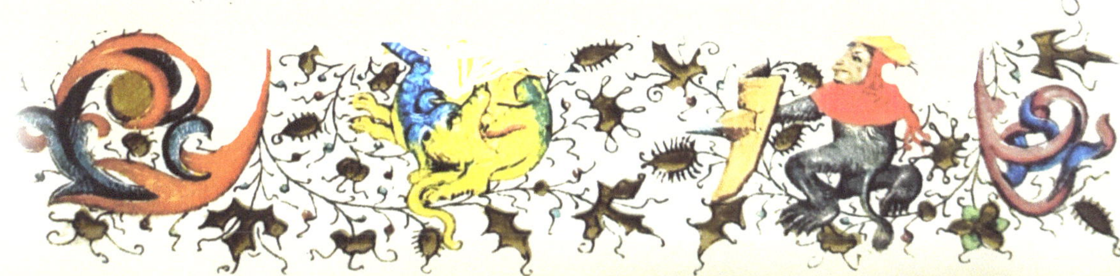

The Crucifixion

Jesus is nailed to the cross and dies in the presence of a crowd full of fear and hatred, blinded by their own pain and sorrow. He cries in compassion, "My God, my God Why have you forsaken me?"
"Father, into your hands I commend my spirit."

Help us, Mary, for we have witnessed too much death. You stood watch at the death of your child, wrongly accused, tortured, and killed. You listened as your Son labored His last breath. You heard His last act of forgiveness and care for the one beside him. Jesus mourns for our Earth.
"Father, forgive them for they know not what they do".

Grace us with awareness. Much of our world hangs lifeless because of our transgressions. Mary, we are contrite for all our participation in war, violence, hatred, and prejudice. Help us to give our lives so that the world we have broken may be healed. We pray on behalf of those who have died, those alive now, and those not yet to be born. He has shown in Himself our guilt with contrition, "Father, if it be thy will, let the Earth be renewed."

OUR FATHER in New Zealand

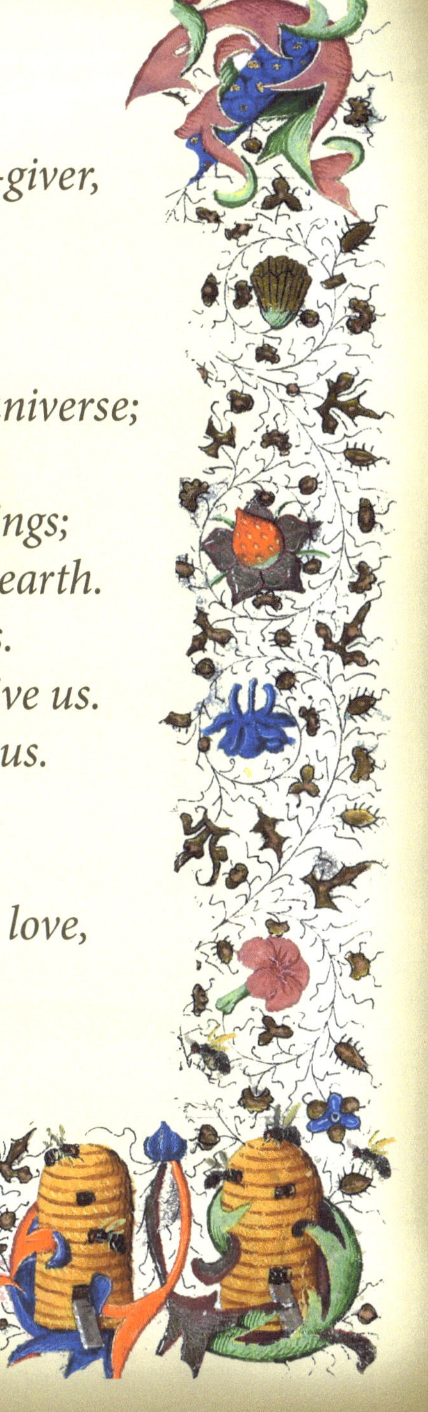

Eternal Spirit, Earth-maker, Pain-bearer, Life-giver,
Source of all that is and that shall be,
Father and Mother of us all,
Loving God, in whom is heaven:
The hallowing of your name echos through the universe;
The way of your justice be followed.
Your heavenly will be done by all created beings;
Your peace and freedom sustains our hope on earth.
With the bread we need for today, feed us.
In the hurts we absorb from one another, forgive us.
In times of temptation and test, strengthen us.
From trials too great to endure, spare us.
From the grip of all that is evil, free us.
For you reign in the glory of the power that is love,
now and forever. Amen.

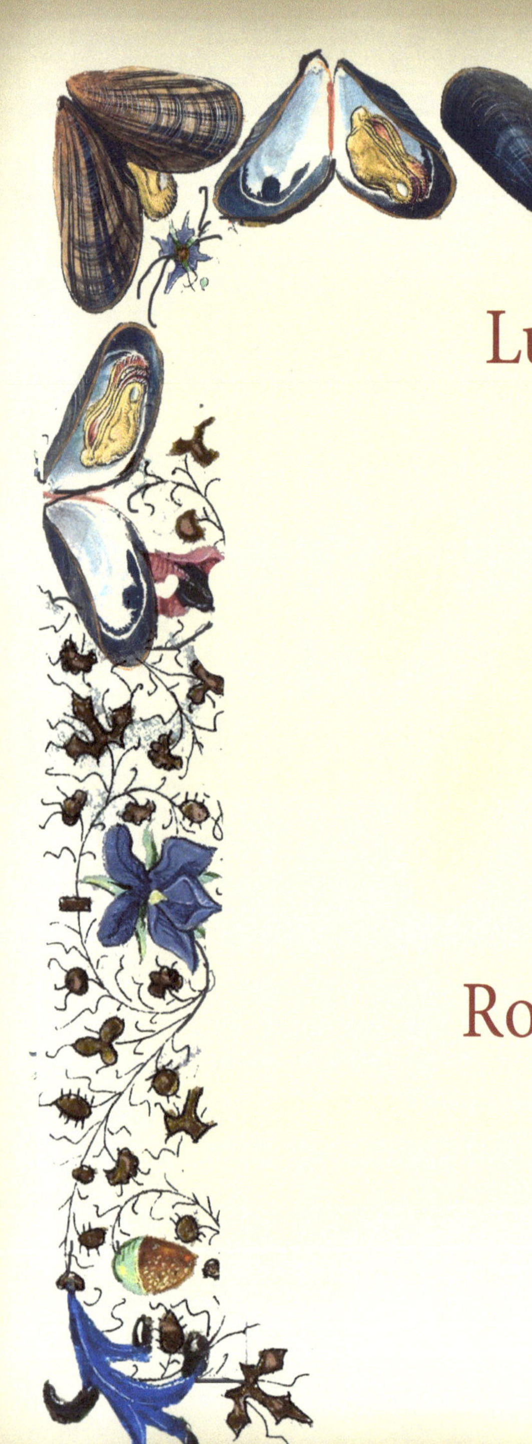

Luminous Mysteries

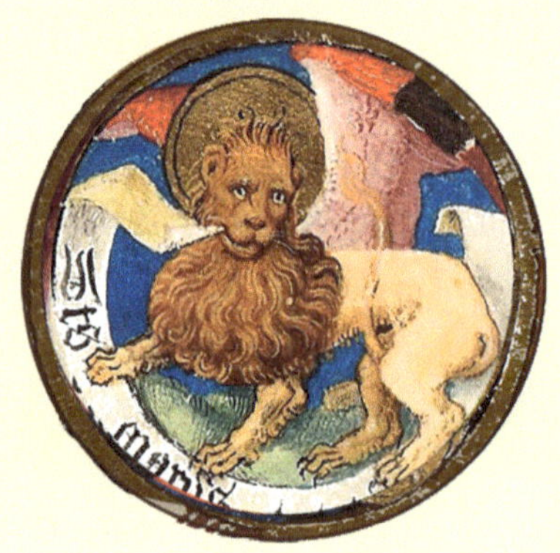

Rosary Meditations of Thanksgiving

Baptism

The Baptism of Jesus in the Waters of River Jordan Let us baptize and be baptized with the Holy Spirit and the Earth's crystal waters.

Help us, Mary, to fulfill our baptismal promises sanctified by the precious waters of the Earth. Grant us the wisdom to recognize water as a sacred element without hindering its natural way of replenishment.

Guide us in protecting and celebrating the transformative nature of water that abounds in oceans and glaciers provided by the Creator. Increase our love for you, the rain-maker, without wasting or polluting what falls from Heaven and fills the ancient aquifers, lakes, and rivers.

We are grateful for the glorious diversity of life sustained by you that abounds on Earth. Illuminate our minds with thanksgiving for God, the Creator of all that is.

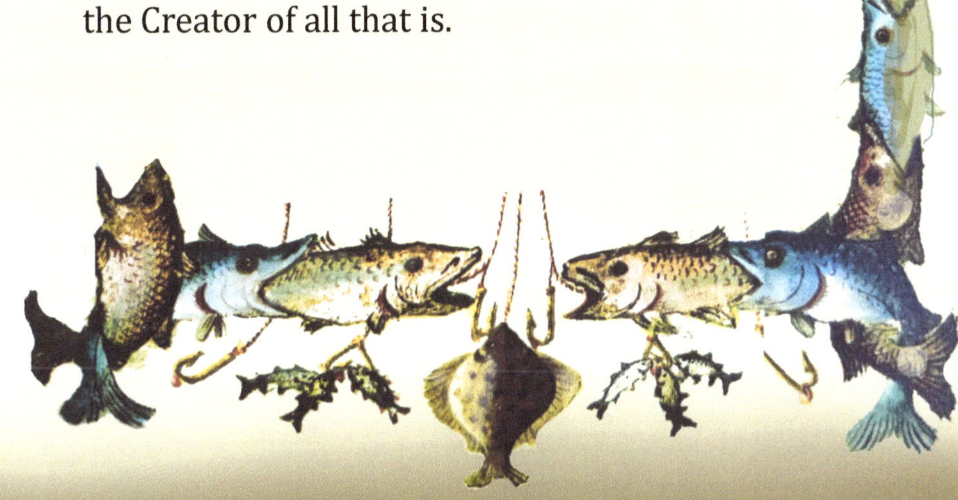

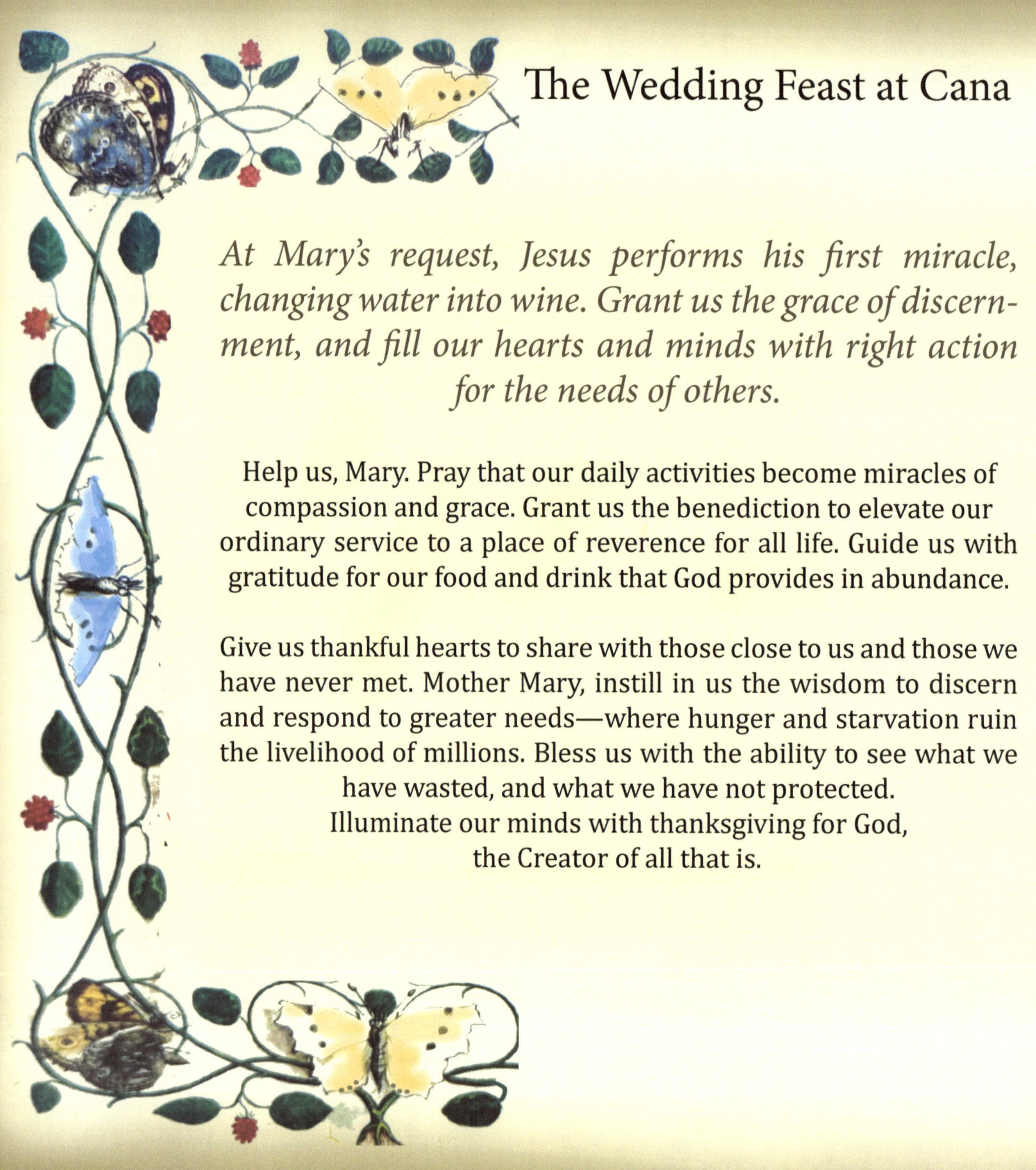

The Wedding Feast at Cana

At Mary's request, Jesus performs his first miracle, changing water into wine. Grant us the grace of discernment, and fill our hearts and minds with right action for the needs of others.

Help us, Mary. Pray that our daily activities become miracles of compassion and grace. Grant us the benediction to elevate our ordinary service to a place of reverence for all life. Guide us with gratitude for our food and drink that God provides in abundance.

Give us thankful hearts to share with those close to us and those we have never met. Mother Mary, instill in us the wisdom to discern and respond to greater needs—where hunger and starvation ruin the livelihood of millions. Bless us with the ability to see what we have wasted, and what we have not protected.
Illuminate our minds with thanksgiving for God,
the Creator of all that is.

The Proclamation of the Kingdom of God

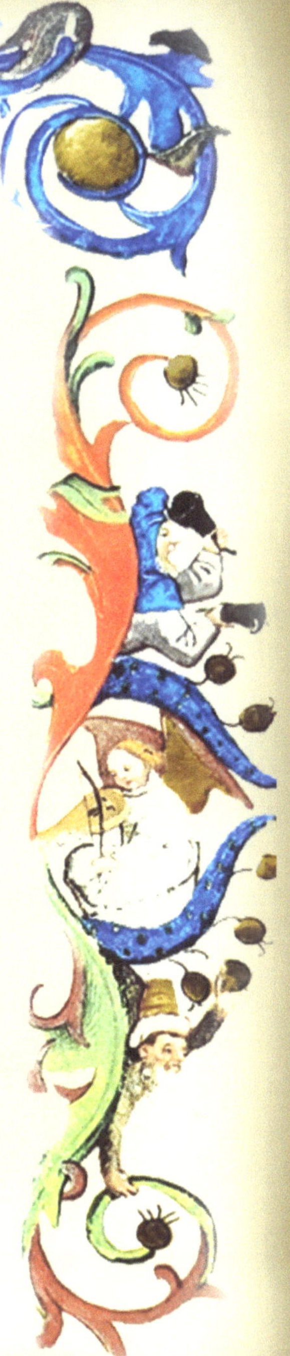

Jesus calls all to serve in the Kingdom of God. Illuminate every mind to resist unrestrained consumption, as we pray that this world will never be depleted.

Pray with us, Mary, thy kingdom come thy will be done, on Earth as it is in heaven. Grant us correct judgment to repair and conserve the environment. Guide us in honoring the energy that courses through Creation, as you knew it so intimately in your womb.

Bless us with the grace to recognize that the time of true fulfillment has come, as we weep in our helplessness. Give us the spirit of repentance for all vice and turn away from destructive pleasures that cannot be upheld by Spirit. Heal us of our insatiable desire for more. Grant us the wisdom to know when we have enough for ourselves and leave the extra for those less fortunate. Illuminate our minds with thanksgiving for God, the Creator of all that is.

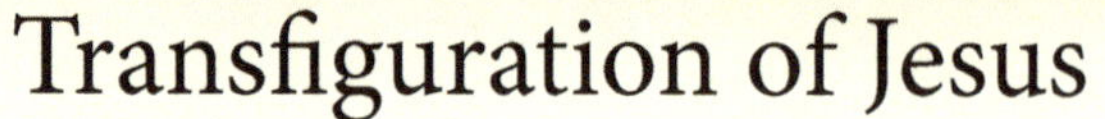

*We are witness and rejoice in
God's transforming power to heal us and the planet.*

Help us, Mary, to see God's glory and the mystery that bathes all of Creation. Mother Mary, you strengthen our hope in God's promise of a New Heaven and a New Earth. Guide us to never forget the power of prayer that transforms us
into people of peace, charity, and justice.

Pray that we are graced with the courage to confront our own doubts and struggles so paramount in this modern era of waste and destruction. Comfort and heal all that has been poisoned by neglect. Bless our efforts, Mary, in faith, hope, and love for one another even when we fail to see

God's glorious transfigurative power in the world.
Illuminate our minds with thanksgiving for God,
the Creator of all that is.

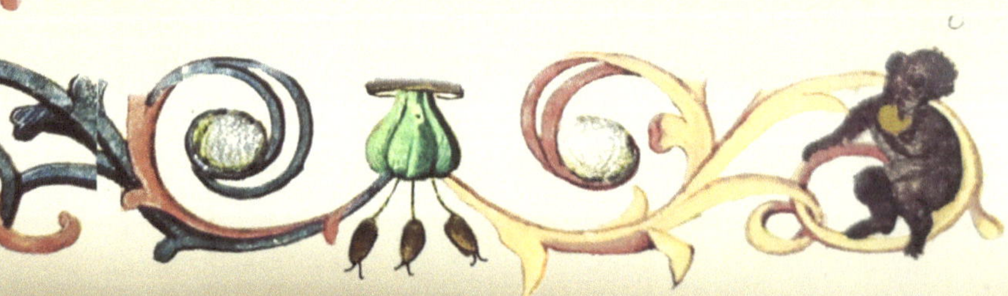

The Institution
of the Eucharist

In communion, let us remember who we are and our connection to the Sacred Earth through the sacrament of His body and blood.

Mother Mary, increase our desire for the sanctified bread and wine offered, the fruits of the earth and the work of human hands.

Grant us a vision of the Eucharist, its sacramental power to arouse our love for one another and the entire cosmos. We say, "take this in memory of me." God has given us His Son and all of Creation to partake of freely. Christ's blood has been poured out for humanity, as mother Earth is generous without limit. Guide us with reverence for all that life offers.

His spirit offers forgiveness for our transgressions, our growth in virtue, and the restoration of humanity around the globe. As children of God, teach us to live life in a new way, as people of peace and generous sharing. Illuminate our minds with thanksgiving for God,
the Creator of all that is.

O God,

*Who resides in divine spaces near and far,
come and make your name Holy among us.*

*May peace and justice be evermore established in your
world, and may your purpose be fulfilled.
Grant us what we need for today,
Forgive us for what we have done to or
neglected to do for others,
And forgive those who have engaged in actions against
us.
Help us to resist the temptations
of fear, hatred, and scapegoating
which harms your creation. Liberate us
from thoughts and actions that demean and
dehumanize that which you love.
Lead us not into temptation but deliver us into your light.*

*For yours is the power shown in extra-ordinary ways,
and the glory that shines through what you have made
and what   will be forever.*

Glorious
Mysteries

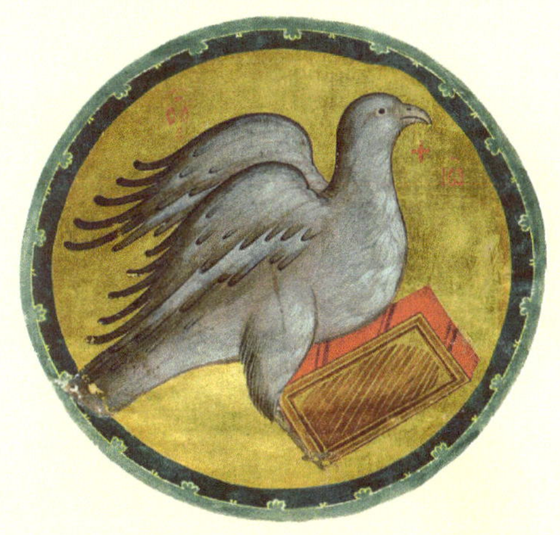

Rosary
Meditations of Petition

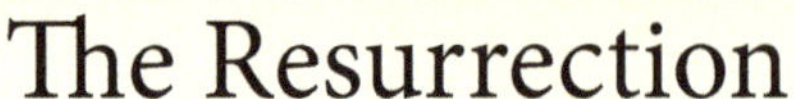

God the Father raised Jesus from the dead. "He is not here. He has risen as He said." "Peace be unto you… do not be afraid." At His resurrection, He appeared to the people, who witnessed and believed in life everlasting.

We have become a new family of believers. Bless us with a vision of Christ's living spirit in our brothers and sisters, regardless of race, religion or language. Mother Mary, you nurtured the unborn Christ within you, and the same risen Christ that nurtures all people, all life, and all creation.

Mighty God, Your crucified and buried Son did not remain in the tomb. Guide us to see the Glory of Your Creation resurrected. Bless us with unrestrained eagerness and fervor for the restoration of our terrestrial home, through Jesus Christ our Lord, who reigns with You and the Holy Spirit, one God, now and forever. Amen. Mary birthed the Christ who breathes through us. We pledge to protect and defend this glorious planet.

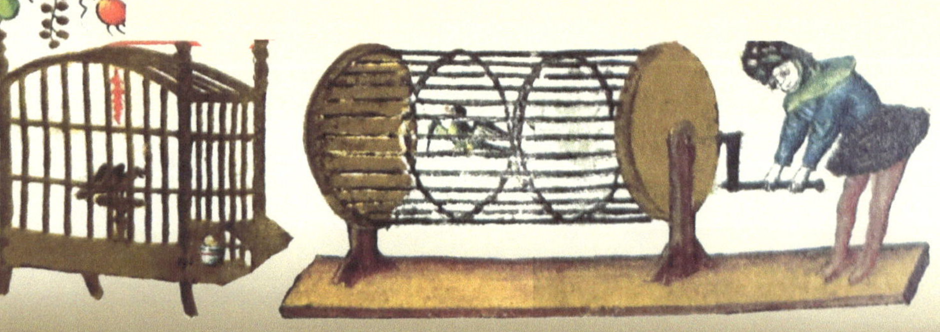

The Ascension

Jesus returns to his Father in heaven. He commissions the apostles to be examples of grace. As He ascends, the wounds in His glorified body are an endless reminder of the harm we have done to one another and the planet.

Help us Mary, to allow God's love for humanity to touch, heal, and affirm a change in our hearts; let the same love ascend to you through Jesus, your son. Let us become resurrected people with Christ, to revere and serve the created order.

Jesus said, 'I am with you for only a short time, and then I am going to the one who sent me.' "Men of Galilee, and all of humanity, why do you stand here looking into the sky? Christ remains here with you in the same way if you believe". Help us realize the magnitude of God's gift; entrusting humankind with his creation.

Mother Mary you were—and are—a reminder that Christ did redeem the created order from within creation, from within your womb. His ascension is sacred cosmology where the origin, evolution, and fate of the universe is in His hands. Mary birthed the Christ who breathes through us. We pledge to protect and defend this glorious planet.

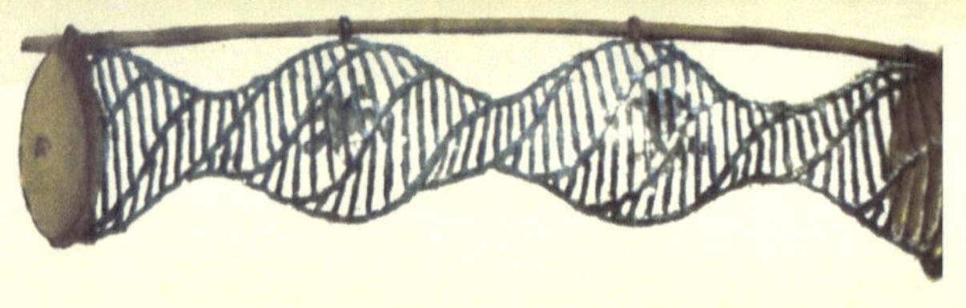

The Coming of the Holy Spirit

The Holy Spirit comes to bring new life to all of humanity. A sound came from heaven like the rush of a mighty wind, and it filled the whole house. The multitudes watched in confusion because every man heard each other speak in his own tongue.

Help us, Mary, to hear the Holy Spirit and rejoice in God, our creator, regardless of our color, race, language, or belief. Guide us to act as stewards of God's creation in all we do, think, and say. Comfort and heal us with the wisdom gained from our childhood traumas, and confess to you our acts of aggression towards one another and the natural order.

Divine spirit, you have promised us healing, even of the scars that we've inflicted on humanity and creation. Bless us with faith and trust that your Holy Spirit will weaken the pride, overshadow the misuse of power, and renew the human heart. Oh Spirit come, life is meant to be lived boundlessly yet without injury to oneself or other. "I will find no rest till I rest in thee".

Mary birthed the Christ who breathes through us and renews in us. We pledge to protect and defend this glorious planet.

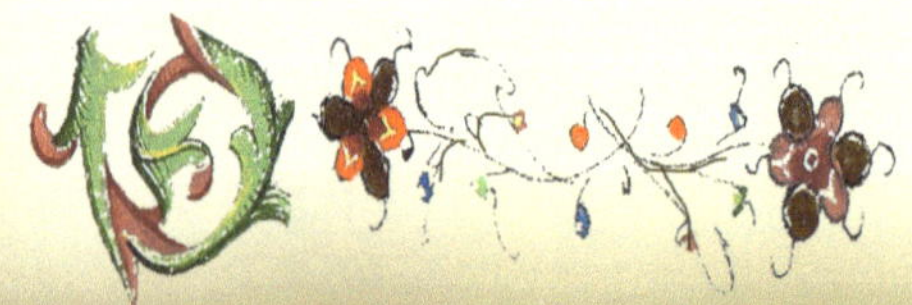

The Assumption of Mary

At the end of her life on earth, Mary is taken body and soul into heaven. She is a source of comfort, consolation and strength to the apostles. She is wholly overcome in a rapture of divine love.

Help us, Mary, to realize the beauty of death and the continuum of life. Pray that your Son grants us the grace to find hope in a troubled world.

Guide us as you gaze from above, make us leaders who protect the Earth's biosphere and celebrate her delicate design. Grant us courage, knowledge, and right action to partake in your nurturing wisdom. Guide us with your spirit to challenge one another, to petition, intercede, and protect life.

Bless us with abundant care for resources and preservation of the Earth's natural balance. Help us understand we have come from divine life and to that same life we return, without end or corruption. Mary birthed the Christ who breathes through us. We pledge to protect and defend this glorious planet.

The Coronation of Mary

Mary is crowned as Queen of Heaven and Earth. Our Mother shares fully in the glory of Christ because she shared fully in His suffering. Her blind trust in God to labor for the wellbeing of all people.

Help us, Mary. The angels and saints longed for Mary's arrival, the female wisdom whose heel crushes the head of the serpent. You are a woman, clothed with the sun, crowned with twelve stars and the moon beneath your feet. Bless the whole world with the grace to see in you a foretaste of the new heavens and the new earth. Grant us Holy Mother to see the awesome power created in you. Humanity has gravely transgressed against the planet.

Our disregard for preserving and protecting God's sacred creation is shameful. We do not deserve His grace. Continue your intercession and miraculous appearances to fortify our fears and anxiety due to our misguided actions and ignominy. Guide us in prayer to act boldly so that the entire human race lives prudently, temperately, and for the benefit of future generations, as it was in the beginning and will be forever.

Mary birthed the Christ who breathes through us. We pledge to protect and defend this glorious planet.

Our Creator

May your Name be on my tongue,
in my thoughts, and the force behind all my actions.
May my will be your will,
as I live and move and have my being.
May my capacity for forgiveness increase daily to realize
life's sacrifice made for me.
May I notice and be grateful this day and every day.
In this world, as it is in your celestial heaven.
Forgive my trespasses as I forgive
those who trespass against me.
And do not let temptation be too powerful to resist
what evil stands before me.
Make me open and conscious of your constant presence
with every thought, word, and deed in my life.
Deliver me from ignorance, sloth, pride, hatred,
gluttony, envy and fear.
For Yours is the kingdom, and the power,
within my very being.
I am yours, you live in me.
Amen

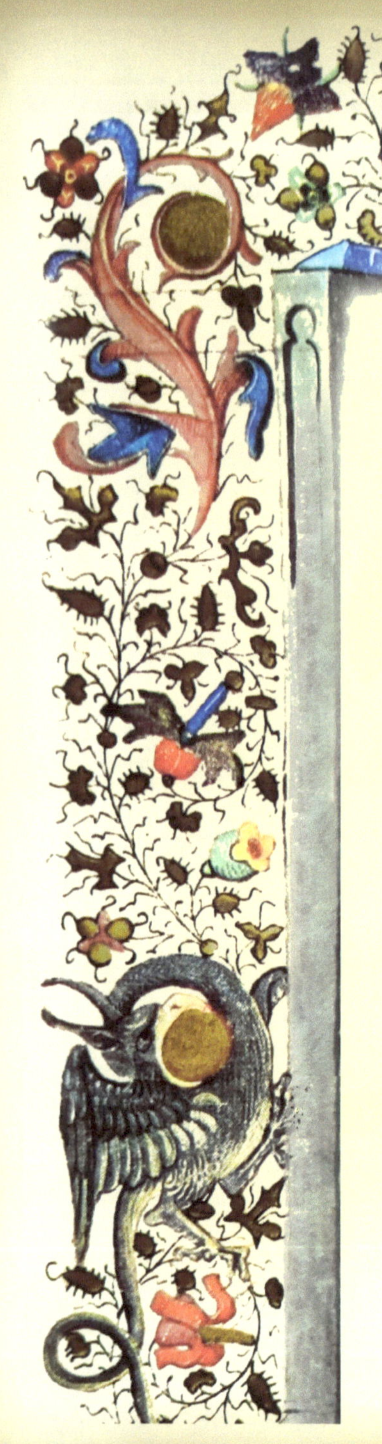

Imagine

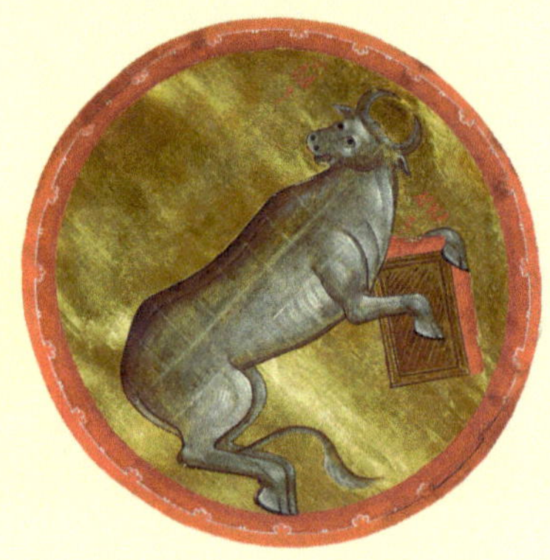

Rosary Meditations
about
Visible Mysteries

Adam and Eve
Genesis 3:22

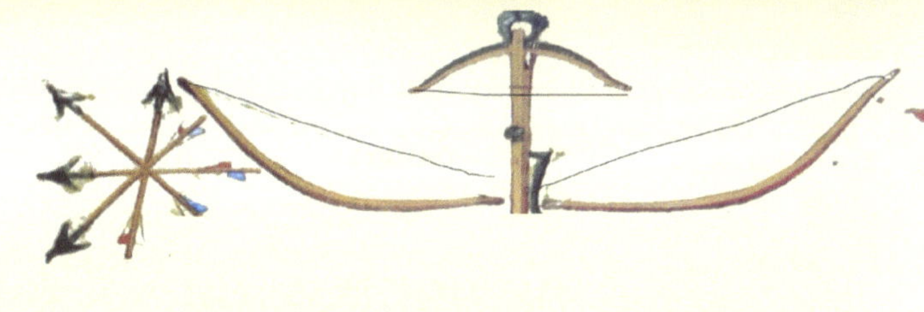

God fashions Adam from earth and places him in the Garden of Eden. Adam is told that he can eat freely of all the trees in the garden, except one. The tree of knowledge of good and evil.

Help us, Mary, to remember we are dependent on the grace of God for our well being. In the beginning God created the Heavens and the Earth and all that is in it. Our Planet was formed from the dust of stars.

Grant us Mary, a redeemed life filled with the miracle of consciousness we have been blessed with. We have taken too freely of God's created order and abused the privilege of our free will. Bestow on us the capacity to know good from evil and alien our lives with Earth's natural harmony.

Comfort and heal us, we weep in our helplessness to turn from our willful-ness, with not enough regard for the divine plan. Mother Mary, teaches us to be independent and free to create as God intended. Holy Mary, Your Son and the Earth have been designed by divine grace and remain visible images of mystery.

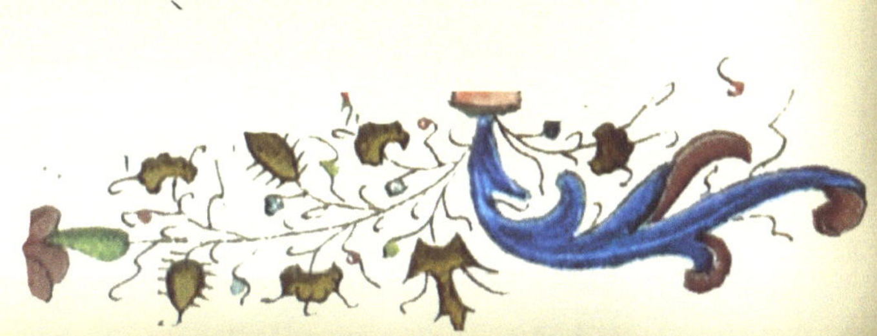

The Mustard Seed
Mark 4: 30–32

The Kingdom of God is like the smallest of seeds and becomes a tree. Living creatures perch in its branches. Our human mind is like a seed planted in the fabric of God's good plan for Creation.

Help us, Mary. In knowing we are chosen and loved by God. Grant us courage, without rank or means to influence a movement of worldwide awareness for the Earth. A handful of visionaries can imagine a world of clean air, crystal clear water and renewable resources. Our majestic history is a source of nourishment and shelter for all who seek the kingdom of God; thy will be done on Earth as in Heaven.

Pray that your Son, who is the ultimate manifestation of love; make us like Him in every aspect. Bless us with the understanding we are one tree, all of the same seed, and our branches are there for the benefit and comfort of all. As one tree we are capable of receiving all the birds from the east, west, north, and south to share wisdom and learning, given to us by grace. Holy Mary, Your Son and the Earth have been designed by grace and remain visible images of divine mystery.

My Ways are not Your Ways
Isaiah 55:8–9

"For my thoughts are not your thoughts, nor your ways are my ways," declares the LORD. "As the heavens are higher than the earth, so are my ways". Help us to transcend our past lies and speak of the Earth's Glory with new tongues.

Help us, Mary, to rest in you as our mother with complete humility and trust in your wisdom and provision. Grant us, committed spirits to love the earth even though we have not learned how. Pray that your Son, whose teachings may confuse our earth-bound minds, teach us to be prophets without fear as life unfolds.

Guide us Holy Mother to see clearly the trauma, abuse, and condemnations that causes our night fears and terrors. Give us a spirit that does not despair from thinking we are insignificant in our capacity to undo the damage we have done. Let us beat on heaven's door for answers to our survival and tragic dilemma. Comfort and heal us, in becoming righteous people, not driven by wickedness or greed.

Holy Mary, Your Son and the Earth have been designed by grace and remain visible images of divine mystery.

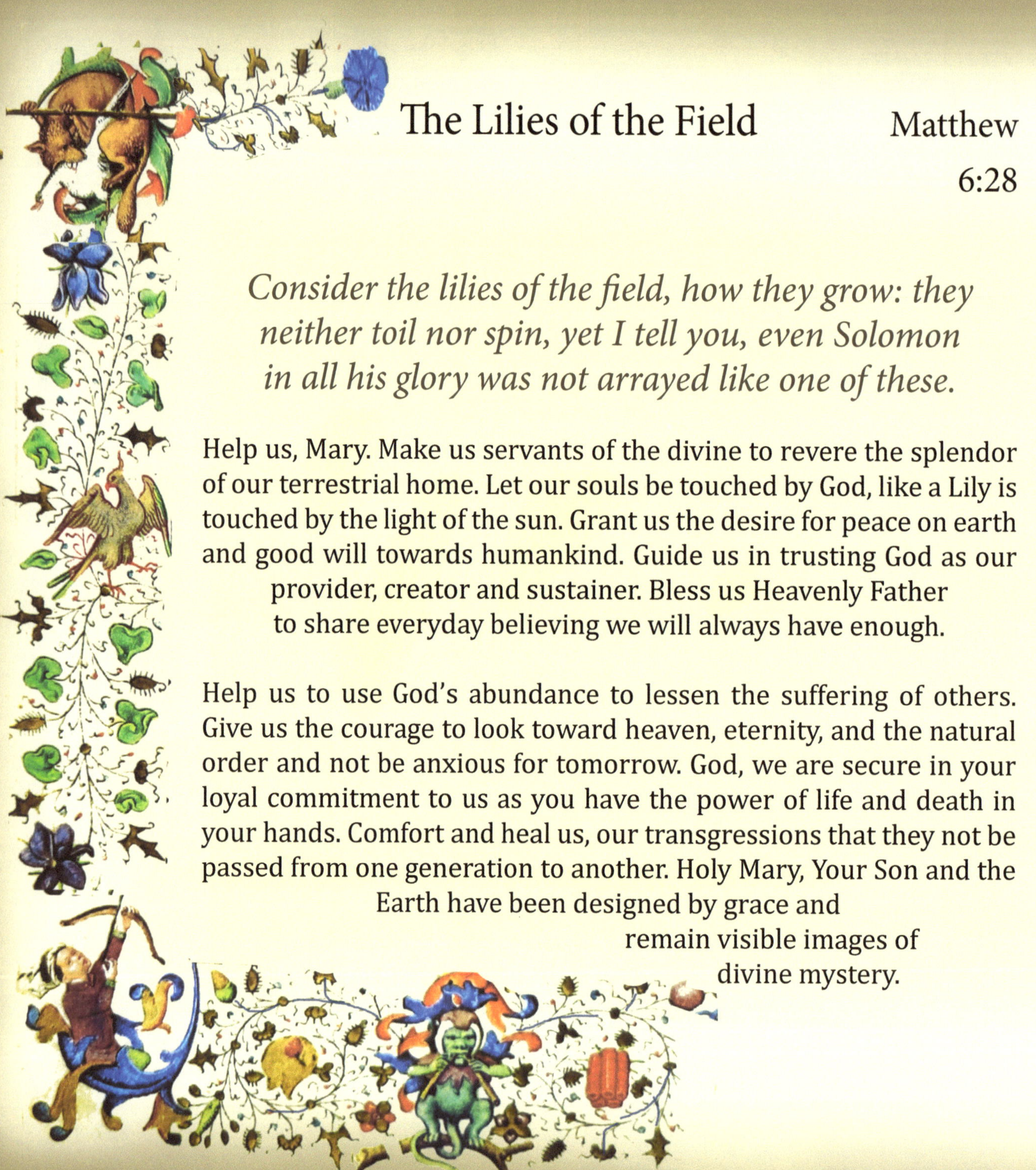

The Lilies of the Field

Matthew 6:28

Consider the lilies of the field, how they grow: they neither toil nor spin, yet I tell you, even Solomon in all his glory was not arrayed like one of these.

Help us, Mary. Make us servants of the divine to revere the splendor of our terrestrial home. Let our souls be touched by God, like a Lily is touched by the light of the sun. Grant us the desire for peace on earth and good will towards humankind. Guide us in trusting God as our provider, creator and sustainer. Bless us Heavenly Father to share everyday believing we will always have enough.

Help us to use God's abundance to lessen the suffering of others. Give us the courage to look toward heaven, eternity, and the natural order and not be anxious for tomorrow. God, we are secure in your loyal commitment to us as you have the power of life and death in your hands. Comfort and heal us, our transgressions that they not be passed from one generation to another. Holy Mary, Your Son and the Earth have been designed by grace and remain visible images of divine mystery.

I Will Always be with You

*Fear not, for I am with you; be not dismayed, for I am
your God; I will strengthen you, I will help you,
I will uphold you with my righteous right hand.*

"We fix our eyes not on what is seen, but on what is unseen, since what is seen is temporary, but what is unseen is eternal" 2 Corinthians 4:18. Give us strong minds and hearts to trust your constant generosity, regardless of circumstance. Help us to dream God's plan of fredom to be fully human, and recall our original beauty along with the original perfection of creation.

In you God, evil turns into good for the salvation of many. Let us awaken to the pain we see is the key for our healing. Teach us to observe all that you have commanded, and behold, you are with us always, to the end of the age. Comfort and heal our blind ignorance and reveal to us your original creation in all its beauty and perfection. Drive our imagination with confidence to imagine our world without darkness, and our souls inseparable from the Creator.

Holy Mary, Your Son and the Earth have been designed
by grace and remain visible images of divine mystery.

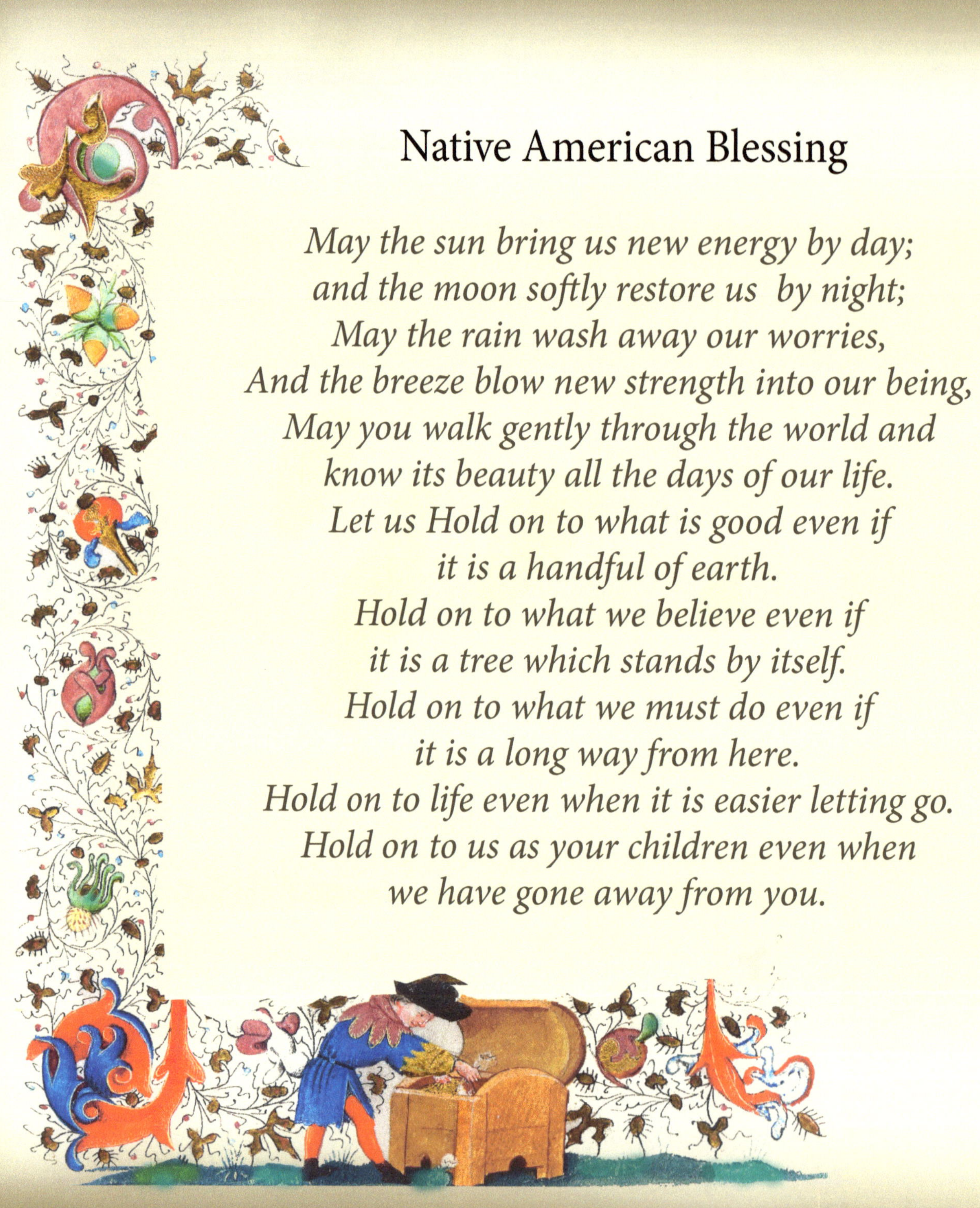

Native American Blessing

May the sun bring us new energy by day;
and the moon softly restore us by night;
May the rain wash away our worries,
And the breeze blow new strength into our being,
May you walk gently through the world and
know its beauty all the days of our life.
Let us Hold on to what is good even if
it is a handful of earth.
Hold on to what we believe even if
it is a tree which stands by itself.
Hold on to what we must do even if
it is a long way from here.
Hold on to life even when it is easier letting go.
Hold on to us as your children even when
we have gone away from you.

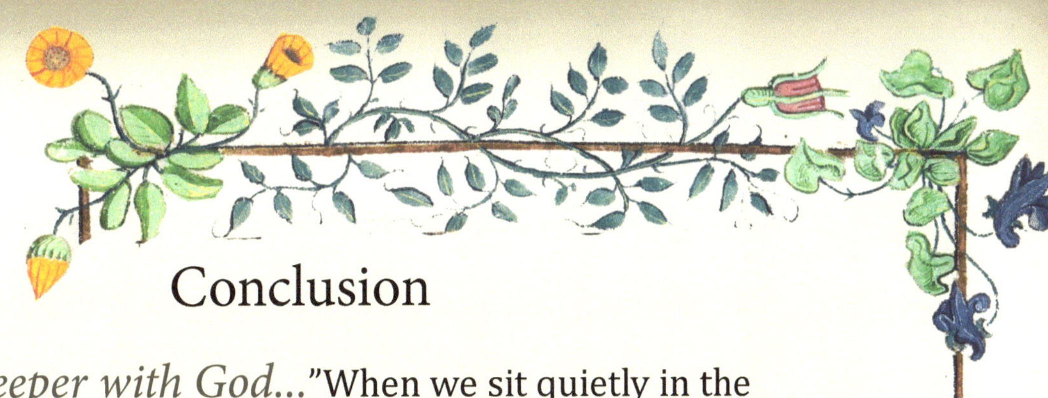

Conclusion

Going deeper with God..."When we sit quietly in the presence of something greater than ourselves, something happens. Desires pour forth, fears subside, and a supernatural calm floods our being. We are being cared for. Praying with Mary through Rosary Meditations opens the door
to God's presence, in our life.

Earth is the Rock upon which we live and move and have our being, a living organism intimately linked and part of us. She breathes, creates and flourishes as we do. Prayer and supplication have been the foundation of spiritual life since the beginning of Christendom. My prayers in this unorthodox book of prayers will hopefully sensitize your heart to the current condition and vulnerability of our planet. We are deminishing her abundance one day at a time like never before in history.

Come alive in the present moment, get fully engaged—body, mind, and spirit—in prayer and communion with God. Let your heart connect with the heart of our Creator. Take this journey, converse and get to know God—Father, Son, and Holy Spirit—
as the One who is ever available,
always present, and ready to listen.

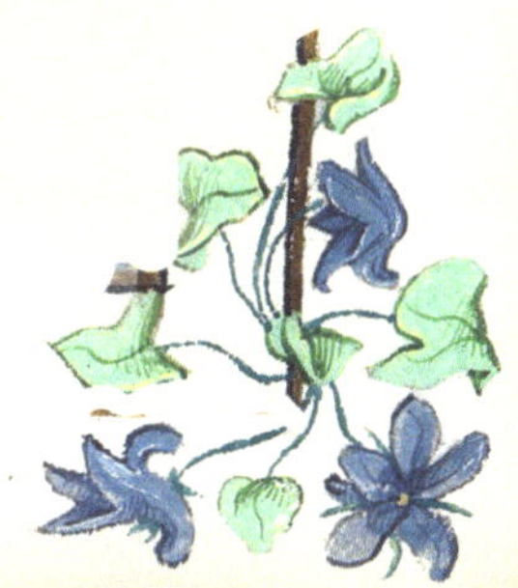

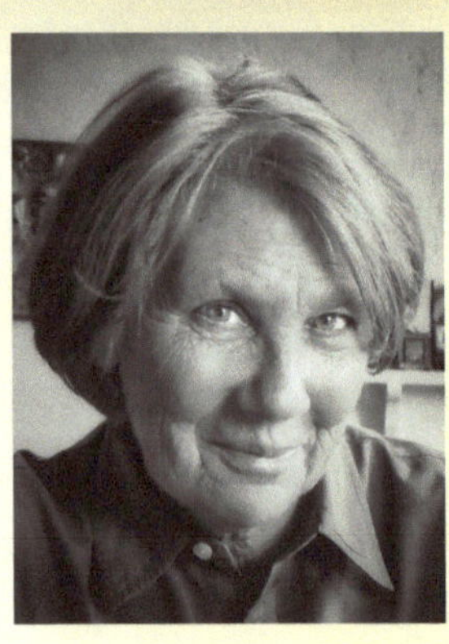

About
the Author

Mary Jane Miller, born 1954 in New York a full time artist and thinker her entire life. She is a self-taught Byzantine style iconographer with over three decades using egg tempera. She has been a prolific painter of sacred art, exhibiting in Museums and churches in both the United States and Mexico. She lives in San Miguel de Allende, Mexico.

Miller is a passionate artist, designer, teacher and author. Her web sites are abundant with information and resources for contemporary icon collectors and students. Her discussions on faith, Christianity and prayer are luxurious, blending historical content, and personal insights to arrive at contemporary conclusions about faith and Byzantine style iconography. As an author, her collections, commentaries and viewpoints are provocative. When she offers her 5 day immersion workshops in the US and Mexico she excels at inspiring the group to think about God and re-frame their love of self and the world.

Please contact her about commissioning work in your church, retreat centers, and private sacred space at home.

Websites:
millericons.com
sacrediconretreat.com
sanmiguelicons.com

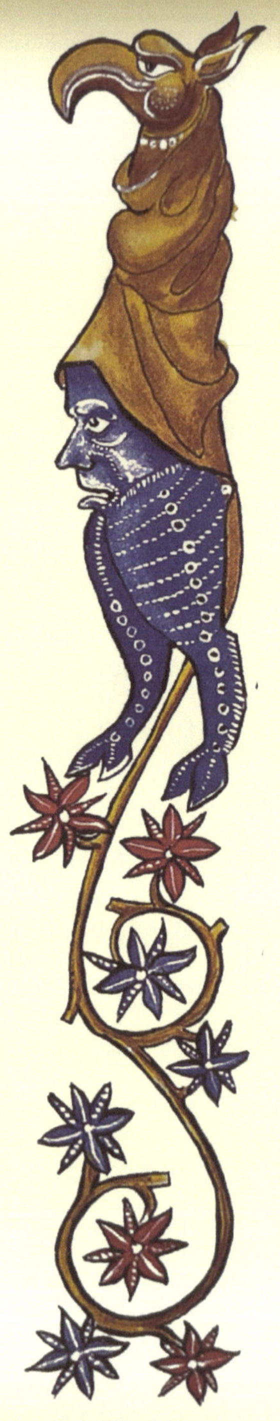

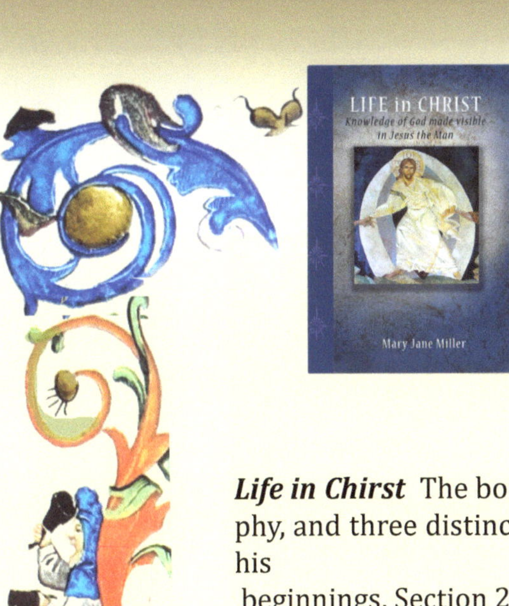
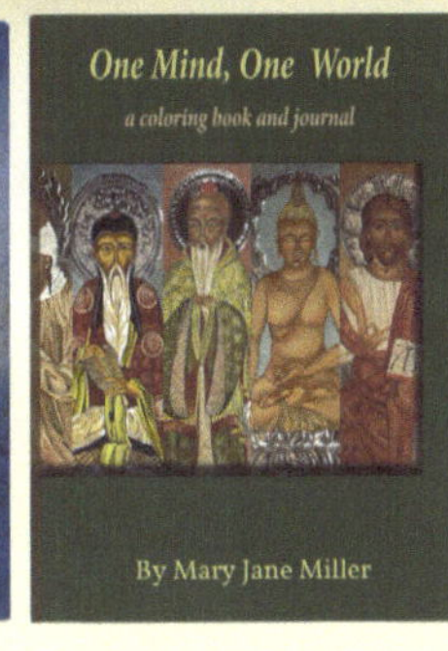
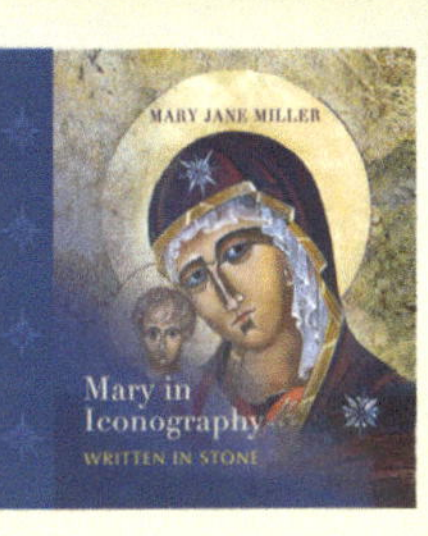
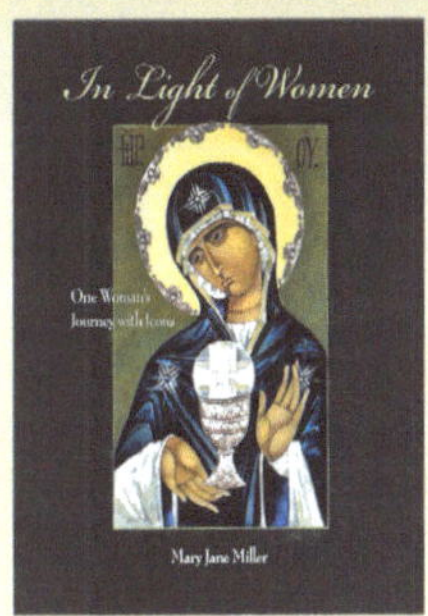
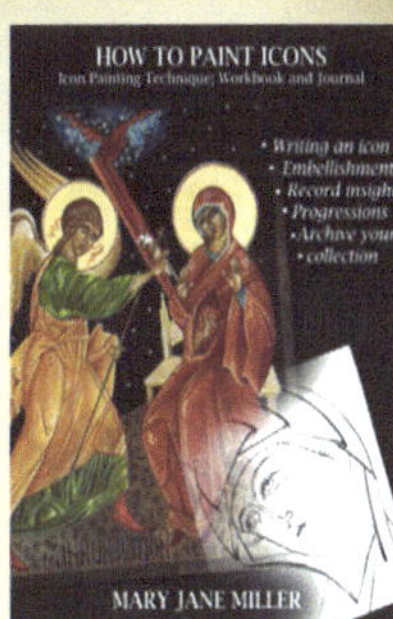

Published Books

Life in Chirst The book includes a Table of Contents, a thorough introduction to iconography, and three distinct sections that build on new conclusions. Section 1, The life of Jesus: his
 beginnings, Section 2, Signs and Wonders: miraculous events witnessed by his disciples, Section 3 Christ: spiritually present and emotionally tangible.

One Mind, One World,   *i*s a coloring book, line drawings from The Dialogue—an art installation with images of great religious leaders and philosophers, who promoted peace on earth and the idea we are all one.

Mary in Iconography,   This collection of Mary icons captures the mysteries of the Madonna, drawing attention to the relationship between Mary and Christ, and the viewer. A wide range of historical documentation, imagination and potential to know Mary the mother of Jesus.

In Light of Women   her collection of women's image in iconography created as an exploration of their voices and portrayal in the church. Vibrant text describing each images history, religiouscontext and her own reflections about the world we live in today.

Icon Painting Technique: A Meditation and Guide to Egg Tempera, explains the subtle relationship between the process of icon painting and how it reflects and enriches one's spiritual life.

Peace be still